A DAY IN THE
COUNTRY
The Pleasures of Rural Life

Doranne Jacobson

SMITHMARK

DEDICATION
This book is dedicated to the country people
of the United States and Canada,
who feed us all and teach us much.

ACKNOWLEDGMENTS
I wish to express my deep appreciation to those who have made it
possible for me to gain insight into the pleasures of life in the country.
Special thanks are due to Elsie B. Novy, Robert L. Novy, Dorothy Novy Wilson,
Russell E. Wilson, Marion Drury, James M. Drury, Lionel Stirrett, Rebecca Stirrett,
and the country people of Michigan, Ontario, New York State, and Illinois.
I also thank Jerome Jacobson for his editorial suggestions.

This edition published in 1994 by SMITHMARK Publishers Inc.,
16 East 32nd Street, New York, NY 10016

SMITHMARK books are available for bulk purchase for sales promotion and premium use.
For details write or call the manager of special sales,
SMITHMARK Publishers Inc.,
16 East 32nd Street, New York, NY 10016; (212) 532-6600.

This book was designed and produced by
Todtri Productions Limited
P.O. Box 20058
New York, NY 10023-1482

Printed and Bound in Singapore

10 9 8 7 6 5 4 3 2 1

Library of Congress Catalog Card Number 94-065424

ISBN 0-8317-0422-5

Author: Doranne Jacobson

Producer: Robert M. Tod
Book Designer: Mark Weinberg
Production Coordinator: Heather Weigel
Photo Editor: Edward Douglas
Editors: Mary Forsell, Joanna Wissinger, & Don Kennison
Design Associate: Jackie Skroczky

Contents

Autumnal golds touch the trees in Peacham, Vermont. White church and red farm buildings assert the hand of humankind amid the natural beauty of the hilly countryside.

Introduction

T*he sun rises through the morning mists, its golden rays sparkling on dew drops clinging to trees and grass. The dawn light illuminates winding lanes, farmhouses, barns, streams, and lakes as it gradually lights up the countryside, waking animals and people to a new day.*

This is the country—rural regions of natural beauty—which we all hold dear somewhere in our hearts. Whether we live in the country or only wish we did, we have all thought a lot about the country and its enduring qualities of tranquil charm and homespun values.

Country life in the United States and Canada has a traditional fascination and allure. We are attracted to these qualities no matter where we live. Life on the land is associated with essential virtues, such as self-sufficiency, the importance of family ties, neighborliness, and strong character tempered by concern for others—principles we all value. The roots of our national heritage are to be found in the countryside, and thus we view country life with increasing affection. We find comfort in the survival, beyond the stresses of urban centers, of cherished folkways and strong beliefs that have stood the test of time.

Hard work and simple pleasures are combined in rural life, both today and in the past. Nature is paramount—the fertility of the soil, the warmth of the sun, the blessings of rain,

Old Glory waves at a New Hampshire town, commemorating the Fourth of July, Independence Day. The nearby gazebo will soon shelter town officials inviting citizens to celebrate the holiday with a picnic and patriotic music.

and the cold snows of winter—affecting country life on a daily basis. For farm men, women, and children, who make a living from the land, there is great pride involved in planting a seed in the earth, caring for it, watching it grow, and harvesting it, all during the course of a challenging and rewarding year. Close involvement with animals is also key—nurturing domestic creatures, even as wild animals live near at hand, is of great concern to many country folk.

The misty light of an autumn dawn in New England illuminates frost on foliage and fence, harbinger of the cold weather to come.

Tied to the land and to one another, country people feed North America and many other parts of the world. Many face times of great difficulty, as prices for land and produce rise and fall, creating stressful economic pressures. Advances in technology and management capabilities have enabled fewer farmers working on larger farms than in the past to produce the food and fibers we need, and many country folk are shifting to a variety of occupations in urban settings. In recent decades, the percentage of the population engaged in agriculture has dwindled dramatically. Yet, out of all proportion to their numbers, country people practice a way of life that greatly influences us all. In these times of change, country people are adjusting to their new circumstances while at the same time living according to time-honored principles of deep and lasting value.

A Day In The Country *takes you on a photographic journey through the seasons in some of the most beautiful country settings in the United States and Canada. You will glimpse lovely rural scenery—mountains, waterways, fields, and forests—as well as settings shaped by human hands—farms, gardens, and country villages and towns. Readers will also encounter animals of the wild in these pages, as well as pets and barnyard livestock. Flowering plants and trees accent country vistas with their seasonal colors. The many facets of country work and pleasures are celebrated in this appreciative portrayal of country life.*

The arrival of winter means beginning preparations for the holidays. In a stand of New England evergreens, a man wields an ax, chopping down a Christmas tree for his family.

Following page: Glacial snows make slippery footing for hikers at Glacier National Park in Montana. At this high altitude, the brisk air is thin but invigorating. The challenge of the climb gives hikers a satisfying encounter with nature at its most elemental.

The Promise of Springtime

The world outside seems chilly and gray, trees still bare, cold ponds still, dark stalks of dead grasses sticking up beside them, damp rotting leaves lying heavy on the ground. The last vestiges of winter's snow have melted, with nothing pretty to take their place, only dismal hues of lifeless nature.

And then you hear it—faint at first, but getting louder—small, shrill sounds of something singing. You listen more attentively; yes, that's it, the songs of the spring peepers. They are tiny brown frogs, so elusive you can seldom see them. But if you put on rubber boots and step slowly into a cold dark woodland pond, you may spot one swimming swiftly away from you. You will note the unusual markings—upon the back a cross of darker brown, giving the animal its name—*Hyla crucifer*—bearer of the cross. Uniquely marked, spring peepers are tree frogs with a special mission: to announce to the awakening world that the frigid months of winter have ended and that spring has come.

Maple Sugaring

The sounds of the spring peeper are preceded by a more silent sign of resurgent life—the flowing of the sap in sugar maples. In many rural areas, from mid-March to mid-April, while nights are still cold but days are warm enough to force the sap to run, the maple trees are tapped. A small hole is drilled in the trunk, a narrow spout of wood or metal inserted, and a bucket hung from the spout to catch the watery flow. The buckets of sap are collected and hauled by horse-drawn wagon—or by snowmobile—to a collecting area. There, in open pans over wood fires, or in spe-

Silhouetted against the spring sky, an Amish farmer in Pennsylvania plows his rich land, optimistically reaffirming his faith that the land will yield a crop to feed himself and his family throughout the coming year.

Beneath arching trees, mists of early morning envelop two Michigan boaters as they move across still waters toward a favorite fishing spot.

cial flat evaporators, the sap is carefully boiled, the water in the sap slowly vaporizing, leaving behind the wonderful essence of the maple tree. It takes about thirty-five gallons of sap boiling for several hours to yield a gallon of syrup. In some areas today, elaborate arrays of plastic tubing channel the sap to centralized tanks and evaporator plants.

My father grew up in central Michigan and spent many weeks each year on his cousin's farm. He often remembered the days of gathering maple sap for syrup as being especially exciting. He joined his cousins in tapping the trees and carrying the buckets brimming with sap back to the barnyard area. There the children helped stir the pans of boiling sap as the heady aroma of maple syrup filled the air and fed their fantasies of home-brewed epicurean delight—a beautiful prelude to spring.

The delicate flavor of warm maple syrup is a unique gift of nature—and of the American Indians, who taught the European settlers how to extract this sweet substance. In recognition of the significance of the sugar maple, four states—New York, Vermont, West Virginia, and Wisconsin—have chosen it as their official state tree. With its extensive stands of sugar maples and ideal weather and soil, northeastern North America remains the only area on earth where maple syrup is produced.

Signs of Life

In the country, as the days warm, signs of the emergence of spring begin to appear everywhere. The icy surfaces of frozen ponds and lakes crack and melt. In damp and swampy woodland areas, layers of last autumn's soggy brown leaves are pierced by the fresh green shoots of skunk cabbage, their leaves gradually unfurling into lush clusters. Birds not seen for months suddenly appear— migratory ducks and geese, as well as robins, their red breasts warm against the still-brown grass.

Nestled among fresh blossoms, a young Canada goose greets a spring day. The return of migratory birds and the hatching of their young signal the beginning of a new life cycle for the countryside.

Birds begin to twitter and collect twigs and threads to build their nests, sure indications that they sense that warmer weather is on the way.

Shooting up from unpromising brown ground are thin green lances of crocus leaves, and then the buds appear, ready to open into delicate circlets of white and purple and yellow. Daffodils and narcissus add their complement of pale golds, and then the tulips burst forth in a brilliant rainbow of colors. Days and nights grow still warmer, and in the bright spring sunshine fruit trees explode with batteries of blossoms in frothy white and pink, bringing joy to the hearts of all who behold them. The perfume of ten thousand flowers fills the air. Lush clusters of purple lilacs send forth their intoxicating fragrance. Bees begin to hum, making their endless rounds from flower to flower, carrying on the cycle of life from one year to another. In the gentle spring showers, chartreuse leaves emerge from buds on every tree, and carpets of grass turn from dull beige to verdant green.

Small brown rabbits with twitching noses emerge from hiding places to nibble the new foliage. Broken shells of pale turquoise robin's eggs drop down from nests filled with peeping baby birds, their mouths agape, waiting for morsels brought to them by parents on the wing.

In the field grass growing tall, you may, if you are fortunate, glimpse a red fox taking food to her den for her kits, or you may sight a white-tailed doe walking with her fawn, dappled like the sunlight drifting through maple branches in new leaf.

In the woods, May apples with umbrellalike leaves grow up on thin stalks from the forest floor, and mush-

The sweet smell of spring inspires a small boy in a garden of bright blooms. Early to flower, tulips bring a rainbow of colors to the warming landscape.

Brilliant red amid a sea of blue, an Indian paintbrush blossom contrasts with lupine flowers. The brilliant colors of wild bouquets are one of the greatest delights brought by warm weather.

Golden mustard blossoms sprinkled on a field of vivid green frame a farmer's tractor busy with spring plowing on a tract of Pennsylvania's fruitful land. Delicate new buds emerge on nearby trees.

rooms of various types appear, sometimes so rapidly it seems as if by magic. Large, round white mushrooms known as puffballs take shape—almost like spongy softballs. With their distinctive shape, these fungal treats can be safely gathered and taken home to be sauteed in fresh butter— unlike other mushrooms that can be deadly to those not well schooled in their identification.

Farmers: A New Season

For North American farmers, spring is much more than a time for aesthetic and spiritual pleasure in the reawakening of nature after winter's sleep. Spring is a time to pay attention to what must be done to prepare for the demands of the growing season ahead. Farm men and women make their living through their ability to respond with sensitivity and caution to the forces of nature around them. Their livelihood depends upon their timely actions, appropriate to the particular conditions of weather and geography in which they find themselves.

Farmers in the United States and Canada are very special people. They spring from extraordinarily hardy stock—pioneer men and women who gave up their places in other lands and took the tremendous step of moving to the great North American continent. There they spread out across the valleys, plains, mountains, and prairies, taking chances, showing impressive initiative, enduring untold hardships, and working strenuously to shape homes and farms out of the wilderness. They could rely only on themselves. There were no well-organized commercial centers or groups of well-entrenched craftsmen upon whom to depend for expert assistance. Instead, the pioneers had to do virtually everything on their own. Willingness to work with their hands, to be independent yet cooperate with their families and neighbors, and to dare to dream were all part of the pioneer farmer experience. These deeply felt values endure in country people today.

Independence and freedom. The words ring out for us across the years, carrying with them strong feelings of pride and accomplishment, legacies of our continent's pioneer past. For independence and freedom from deprivation and meddlesome tyrants on thrones and in pulpits, immigrants to our land have always been willing to pay a great price. They have paid with their blood and their toil, often facing insecurity and death, but ultimately creating great nations idealizing democracy and individual opportunity. And for all that has been accomplished, none of it would have been possible without the arduous labors of the people of the land, country people, growers of the crops upon which everyone ultimately depends.

We have no illusions here about the greatness of princes and kings in shaping our nations. We know that it is the common folk, working in the countryside in harmony and in struggle with the forces of nature, who are responsible for laying the groundwork for the things we hold most dear. Happy and healthy families, stalwart homes, and worshipful communities, all prospering in settings of natural beauty—these are what we value and what the efforts of country people have made possible over many decades.

Claiming the Land

As they moved out across the land, settlers blocked out their farms in such a way that each house was far from the homes of neighbors. Each house was set upon its own homestead, surrounded by the family fields. Unlike European and Asian farming communities, where houses tend to be bunched together in villages with agricultural fields surrounding each settlement, North Americans dispersed their homes, ensuring greater independence for each family, and making it necessary for farmers to be expert in many skills.

With green grass just beyond its reach, a young calf gazes from its barnyard pen in New England. Weathered planks and painted wooden siding bear witness to a farm family's labors over many years.

Self-sufficient farmers have long been responsible for building their own houses and producing their own food. The farmer is plower and planter, breeder of cattle, sheep, pigs, horses and poultry, mechanic, carpenter, roofer, wood-chopper, water-hauler, veterinarian, inventor, and, today, computer wizard. The farmer's wife is similarly strong—equal partner with her husband in their joint enterprise. She runs equipment, handles calves and lambs in freezing weather, cans fruit and vegetables to feed the family for the winter, and tends her garden and her children, all while keeping the books, cooking huge meals, and, in her spare time, sewing clothing and quilts.

A Country Childhood

Country children, too, make their essential contributions. As soon as they are old enough, children feed the animals, clean barn stalls, pluck insect pests and weeds from the garden, and begin to take on adult responsibilities. They learn early the importance of the weather and the changing of the seasons and what these can mean to their family's prosperity. There is no question of forcing them to work; like those around them, they see jobs that must be done, and they turn to their chores with a willingness to complete the tasks at hand.

In the countryside, children are not isolated from their parents. They are involved with every phase of farm activity, and they aid adults at every step. Even the young child carries snacks and messages to the father in the field and stands at the mother's elbow in the house, observing the hard work necessary to sustain the family's life. A child as young as twelve or thirteen might be deeply involved in working with animals and machinery on the farm. In rural areas, the timing of school vacations reflects the agricultural cycle, so that young family members can help with seasonal work. As one farmer observed, "One of the best things about farming is that you've got your wife and kids and work all wrapped together, all in one spot, all at home. You can't have that in many other businesses."

Just as family life is treasured among rural people, neighborliness is highly valued. My friend Lionel Stirrett, who grew up on a farm in central Illinois but now lives in a city, remembers with nostalgia the help and companionship that farmer neighbors gave each other in his youth in rural central Illinois:

Gathering pink petals fallen from a magnolia tree in full blossom, a young girl dressed in Easter finery fills a basket with beauty before it can slip away.

> When we were growing up, there was a group of us that got together once a month to play pinochle—a group of neighbors. And in the summer when we were harvesting the forages—the hay—the neighbors all worked together. They exchanged help; six or seven neighbors would all work together. ... Here in the city, the neighborliness is one of the things that you miss. ... Part of it is that we're not tied as much through need as they were on the farm. Here it's not a livelihood situation.
>
> You know, even today, if you hear that a farmer's sick, twenty-five farmers will go in and harvest his crops for him for free. At times they're very competitive with one another, but if someone has troubles, they respond very quickly. When we were kids and a farmer had a heart attack or something like that, the neighbors would all go in and help with the crops. In fact, when my dad died ten years ago, the neighbors came and planted crops for us. They came in and harvested the crop too.

Right:
Fishing for trout in a Wyoming stream, young boys experience the special satisfaction of interacting closely with nature. Fishing is one of the most popular forms of recreation for people of all ages.

Time-Honored Methods

Imbued with an especially deep sense of family and community are the Pennsylvania Dutch, descendants of Amish and Mennonite settlers who came to Pennsylvania in the 1600s and 1700s from German-speaking areas of Europe. (They are called Dutch because the word *Deutsch*, which means German, was misinterpreted.) Sometimes called the "plain people," they sought freedom to practice their devout Protestant faith and live simply, according to pious precepts, in tightly

knit farming communities. They are now prosperous farmers in many regions of the United States and Canada and some countries of Latin America.

The Old Order Amish are especially conservative, teaching peaceful separation from the world. The men wear beards and wide-brimmed hats, while the women wear bonnets and long dresses. (In their view, the dress of non-Amish is ugly and strange.) The Amish till the soil with horses and mules and refrain from using electricity or telephones. They are famous for helping each other with barn-raisings and other activities. Their farms are models of success achieved through hard work, cooperation, and old-fashioned methods.

When farm folk sense that spring is in the air, they move quickly to prepare for the season's change of pace. As snow melts away from fields, the farmer walks the edges of his land, searching for fences that need mending. He and his boy go out to make repairs, knowing that grazing animals will soon be seeking weak spots in the fences that hem them in. Metal and wooden posts tipped askew by the heaves of winter's frosts are set straight and pounded firmly into the earth again, and loose fencing is pulled taut or replaced. On farms with zigzag cedar fences, where snowdrifts have pushed the split logs aside, the farmer sets these aright, aligning the weathered, silvery wooden rails one upon the other as generations of farmers have done before him. At the same time, along the road in front of the house, the metal rural mailbox is checked. If a winter snowplow has knocked its wooden post crooked, it is reset to stand up straight, ready to receive letters and parcels from near and far. The name painted on the mailbox proudly announces to all who pass by the identity of those who work the land.

With fences newly intact and green shoots sprouting from the ground, the time has come to put the livestock out to pasture. Eager cattle, horses, sheep, and even pigs are freed from barn stalls and encouraged to seek their meals outdoors. This lightens the animals' spirits—and instantly reduces the need to clean manure from the barns.

A young girl feeds a thirsty calf from a bottle. Caring for animals is a never-ending responsibility for farmers who keep livestock. As they begin life, young animals often need extra attention to assure a healthy start.

In the Eastern woodlands, young brothers admire a lush cluster of white trilliums. These increasingly rare wildflowers bloom only in damp, shady woods.

Planting

In springtime's sunlight, the fields are warm and ready for planting. Winter's frosts are banished, and the fertile ground must be prepared to receive seed and to give new life. Using tractors pulling various implements, the farmer makes several trips over the ground—more in spring than in any other season.

Several passes must be made to ready the soil for seed. As spring begins, most fields are still covered with the remnants of stalks and stubble from last fall's crop. These must be chopped and blended into the soil, which itself must be loosened and cut fine so that soft rain can seep through to nourish the tender roots of growing plants. Farmers traverse each field with plows and disks which have a variety of teeth, claws, and cutting plates carefully designed for their manifold tasks. Today, most farmers use tractors to pull these implements, but the Old Order Amish stick to traditional teams of horses or mules to power their plows. As fields are tilled, pungent earthy smells rise from the damp furrows, reminding the farmer of his intimate bonds with nature.

Today's farmers are well informed on various ever-changing methods of fertilizing, weed control, and preserving the soil's strength through conservation tillage, reduced tillage, and no-tillage techniques. Hybrid seeds, strip-cropping, crop rotation, as well as organic and nonorganic farming are all considered. Each system has its advantages and disadvantages in different locales, and those who make their living from the land pay close attention to the details of each innovation in agriculture and its potential effects on their families.

For the farmer planting his crop, timing is essential. He watches the sky and reads the clouds and bets with or against the weather. Success depends to some extent on luck, but it also depends upon the farmer's instincts, born of his experience with the land.

Most crops, such as spring wheat, corn, barley, oats, and soybeans, are planted in the spring, the seeds dropped into furrows in the warming earth through the seed drill, drawn across the landscape by a tractor—or, for the Amish, a team of draft animals. The fertile soil closes over the seeds and begins to incubate them for their new surge of life.

Gardens, too, are planted—seeds carefully placed in rows in well-tilled earth not far from country houses. Soon sprouts appear—tiny infant plants destined to yield tasty vegetables to add to family dinners.

With spring iris blossoms in full flower all around him, a boy in central Illinois plants bulbs for next year's floral display. Like other country young people, this youth learns skills necessary for successfully growing plants.

A stalwart team of mules provides the power to pull an Amish farmer's plow through the fertile soil of his Lancaster, Pennsylvania, farm. Amish traditions stress reliance on time-tested methods of agriculture.

A young white-tailed fawn stands on unsteady feet, ready to explore the world. After being hidden in a secluded spot for a month after birth, the fawn begins to follow its mother, who will care for the young animal for more than a year.

White-tailed does nuzzle each other in the cool waters of a spring pond. After the snows of winter, newly green lily pads provide the deer with succulent snacks. Unseen at their feet, tadpoles and other water creatures stir to life.

With his crops safely planted, for the next few months the farmer waits, keeping a careful eye on the health of the growing plants and at the same time constantly watching the weather, always hopeful that the combination will be right to produce a bountiful crop. Country people continuously affirm their intimate connection with nature and the land. Yet, even as they are bound to the forces of nature in a specific small locale, country people are also inextricably enmeshed in the international economy, as prices of crops and land rise and fall in response to a multitude of economic forces at play around the globe.

But attention is always drawn to matters close at hand. Spring lambs are born, and calves meet the world for the first time. Small piglets appear in farrowing houses, and goats bleat for their rations. Tiny kittens and newborn puppies tumble about barnyards, and fresh colts stand knock-kneed at their mothers' sides. Life asserts itself everywhere in the springtime, tangibly expressing hope that there is a future well worth living for all who inhabit the countryside.

Following page:
Scarlet barns
trimmed in
white reveal
a family's pride
on a farm in
Michigan.
Spring's ver-
dant green
shoots hold
promise for a
prosperous agri-
cultural season.

Cherry trees
burst into balmy
bloom in north-
ern Michigan.
Spring breezes
stir the windmill
to pump life-giv-
ing water to the
orchard, ensuring
a bountiful crop
of luscious fruit.

A vivid rainbow trout emerges from the chill April waters of the Madison River in Montana, tugged from its wet lair by an ardent angler. The rosy band along the side of the body gives the fish its name.

A brown trout, also a denizen of Montana's Madison River, displays its spots. Increasingly, enthusiastic fishermen catch fish and then release them, allowing them to continue their lives.

Fragrant flowers on a fruit tree frame a country home in Vermont. Piled stones bespeak a rugged land which yields its bounty only to those willing to work long hours and find pleasure in simple things.

The Pleasures of Summer

A summer's day dawns bright and clear, sunlight filtering through lush leaves in woodlands and shining full on open ground, lighting wild red strawberries, tiny promises of sweetness under low clusters of serrated green leaves. Bird songs fill the air, and fish leap in ponds and streams. Summer pleasures await those who wake to the day in the countryside.

Even the tasks of summer are lightened by the season. Warm weather and long hours of daylight mean that chores can readily be accomplished, leaving time for pleasure before the sun sets. For children, school is out, and after chores, many hours are free for summer pastimes.

Hoeing and weeding gardens, washing clothes and hanging them to dry on clotheslines in the fresh country air, repairing barn doors and walls, scrubbing wooden floors, polishing kerosene lanterns, painting wooden gingerbread trim on Victorian porches, chinking holes in house walls to keep mice outside, replacing cracked window panes, pruning hedges, and admiring zinnias in brilliant bloom in flower beds are all activities for country summer days.

Grasshoppers and crickets chirping in fields of long grass, and cattle lowing softly as they graze in green pastures during the day and gather at the pond for their evening drink are essential summer sounds. Cicadas sing unseen in the trees, and butterflies silently flash their colors below. The air is often cool in the morning, hot at noon, sweltering in the afternoon, and cool again after sunset. In summer, nature is at the height of its fecundity, inviting country people to see, hear, touch, and feel its every mood in intimate interaction.

Summer's carefree days bring joy to a child swinging from a rope tied to a tree. The songs of birds, the chirps of crickets, and the drone of locusts surround the child with the contentment of a country afternoon.

Brilliantly colored balloons rise at the Balloonfest world competition outside of Battle Creek, Michigan. Near the city made famous by Kellogg's cereals—crunchy symbols of wholesome country values—the balloons hark back to times when human flight was barely more than a fantasy.

A woodland glen inspires the magic of music in a young musician. The sound of her French horn blends with the melodies of nature to create a country symphony amid the verdant trees and ferns.

The Ferris wheel spins swiftly, thrilling riders at the annual country fair at Topsfield, Massachusetts. Thousands of fairgoers from city and country alike enjoy the festival atmosphere of this popular fair.

The Animal World

The young animals are growing, needing to be tended, along with older domestic creatures. Pets and livestock give lively character and strength to country homes, especially in summer, when people and animals can enjoy each other the most. Foremost among these are dogs—companions and helpers to those who live on the land. No country child can imagine growing up without a dog, or even several dogs, all named, each with an individual personality, each beloved in his or her own way. A dog stands guard over its people and property, barking to warn off troublesome skunks, raccoons, bears, snakes, and strange people. A dog helps herd sheep or cattle and, in fall, flushes pheasants and quail from tall grasses.

Country cats may come and go, independent as they are, but a dog is a dependable friend over many years. A dog accompanies a child or an adult into a dark barn or along a path into the woods, running about and exploring yet always returning to the person's side, acting as a devoted link between humanity and the rest of the animal world. It is no wonder that faithful dogs are but reluctantly allowed to go to their eternal rest, and their names live on in memory for many years after they are gone.

Goats, horses, sheep, cattle, pigs, poultry, and mules also have their places on farms, their young

With a quivering snout poking from its pen, a pig on rustic Monhegan Island, Maine, greets a visitor. Unable to sweat like most mammals, pigs need shade and mud to help themselves stay cool. Underappreciated, pigs often show surprising intelligence.

Black faces and feet contrast with thick white fleece on a pair of Suffolk sheep peeking from a barn doorway. Docile animals, sheep provide one of nature's finest fibers, useful in a multitude of garments and other products.

A great horned owl perches on a downspout, apparently unafraid of human habitation. With a wingspan of nearly five feet, great horned owls fly so silently that their prey scarcely sense their approach before it is too late.

A haunting reminder of years gone by, a girl from an antique advertisement gazes from the past through a garage window in Arizona. A more sprightly kitten surveys the present from its windowsill seat.

Peering from its own private window in its barn stall, a horse enjoys the fresh country air. Carrying riders, drawing plows, and grazing in green fields, horses contribute quiet strength to rural life.

growing stronger with each passing day of summer. Some are more distant from human affection than others, but each makes its contribution to country life.

Cattle are especially important—there are more than 113 million of them in the United States and Canada. Beef and dairy cattle are raised to supply meat and milk to profit their attentive owners, who in turn provide the animals with pasture, feed, water, and shelter. People sometimes give them names—but cattle do not seem to recognize their names as dogs and horses do. Pigs are also popular barnyard animals—there are some 67 million of them living on Canadian and American farms—and, although they make intelligent pets, most of them are fated to provide pork for human consumption. At one time, most family farms grew crops and raised a few cattle, pigs, and chickens as well, but at present, these animals are more often raised in large numbers on specialized farms. These days, in some areas, one can glimpse exotic animals in North American barnyards—most notably llamas, and even a few camels.

People often develop personal relationships with horses. Over uncounted centuries, horses have been among the most useful animals to country people. In ages past, horses provided the fastest and surest way to travel on land. Brought to the New World by the Spanish, horses carried Native Americans and European soldiers and settlers on their backs across North America. They pulled stagecoaches and covered wagons for pioneers moving westward across the continent. As the plains and prairies were settled, horses drew plows through the heavy turf, pulled wagons and buggies, and carried cowboys driving cattle. Later, they even pulled streetcars and trains on short hauls. Until very recent decades, the horse-drawn milk wagon was a fixture in many towns, the clip-clop of the horse's hooves on the road waking children from their pre-dawn slumbers.

A crowing rooster claims a Vermont porch for his own. Essential adjuncts to country houses, porches provide inviting places for family and friends to meet and share a glass of lemonade or a lively conversation.

With iridescent feathers shining in the sunshine, a black-breasted red game rooster struts down the walkway from his coop. Despite their relatively small size, specially bred game chickens are noted for their strength and vigor.

With the development of motorized vehicles, the prominence of horses as draft animals declined. In 1910, American farmers owned some twenty million farm horses, but by the early 1990s, there were only about six million horses in the United States and Canada. Old horse harnesses and horseshoes hang unused and dusty on many venerable barn walls. Still, farmers hewing to well-tested tradition depend on horses, or mules (cross-bred from a horse and a donkey), using these stalwart animals to draw plows, carts, and carriages. In areas heavily settled by Amish and Mennonite farmers, horse-drawn carriages are a common sight on country roads today, each carriage marked at the back with a fluorescent red triangle to signal caution to automobile drivers driving past in a hurry.

For me, the sight of a horse-drawn carriage evokes family memories of my great-grandparents, who were country doctors in Ohio at the turn of the century. My grandmother often spoke of riding through the countryside at her father's side when she was a child:

> Whenever [my father] was going out on a country drive, as he did all the time, I was bundled up and went along with him. And while I was with him I learned a lot of little songs... he'd laugh at things and show me things along the way. He always had two horses, and when one was dragged out, he came in and was hitched up to another one. Sometimes Mother went off in one buggy and he in the other. Mother drove and was very familiar with horses.

Powerful workhorses pull a wagon for a farmer in Huntington, Vermont. Farmers following old-time methods have long depended on horses for drawing carts, wagons, carriages, and even sleighs.

An Amish farmer drives his mules across his Pennsylvania farm, applying chemicals to the growing crops. While many Amish prefer not to use motor-driven machinery, they know the value of enhancing their farm yields with modern chemicals.

Following page: Twilight's dusky glow illuminates a herd of cattle in a classic moment of country tranquility. Many cattle fend for themselves for months in summer pastures but need deliveries of extra hay in the winter season.

A curious goat inspects its surroundings at a farm in Vermont. This Toggenburg goat is of a European variety known for its nutritious milk. Always energetic, goats are often trained as pets and can be harnessed to children's carts.

A proud equine and its owner emerge from a Vermont barn, ready to get to work. This horse has been specially bred for farm work and is both gentle and strong.

Texas longhorn cattle are hardy and fierce and can protect themselves from predators such as mountain lions and coyotes. Now largely replaced by gentler breeds, longhorns are making a comeback in places like south Texas, where they roam freely over huge ranges.

The horse made country doctors' work possible, carrying them to the far-flung rural homes of their patients in all weather fair and foul, helping to save lives and knit the rural community together. My grandmother recalled that her parents worked as a team, with her father doing all the surgery and her mother administering the anesthetic and dressing the wounds. Either might deliver a baby:

> After a baby was delivered, my mother went for two weeks afterwards—washed and dressed the baby, combed the mother's hair, and made everything comfortable. She got ten dollars for the effort. Half the babies in our county were named after my parents or me. I always had to carry the little namesakes yardage of linen and lace, so they could make a special dress for the child. I had to be the one to go and present it. Every namesake got a gift.

Branding a calf for easy identification occupies workers at a Wyoming ranch. Brands are respected as marks of ownership throughout the West. In early days, tampering with another owner's brand on an animal was met with stern justice.

The horse-drawn buggy was also used for pleasure outings.

> Once I was taken to the circus over in Wauseon. They took me and a little boy who was my playmate, Willy. We had to get up very early and leave in the dark to get there, because it was a twenty-mile drive. We got there just as the circus parade was coming down the street. And the horse, who was desperately afraid of the elephants, simply squatted in its tracks and trembled!

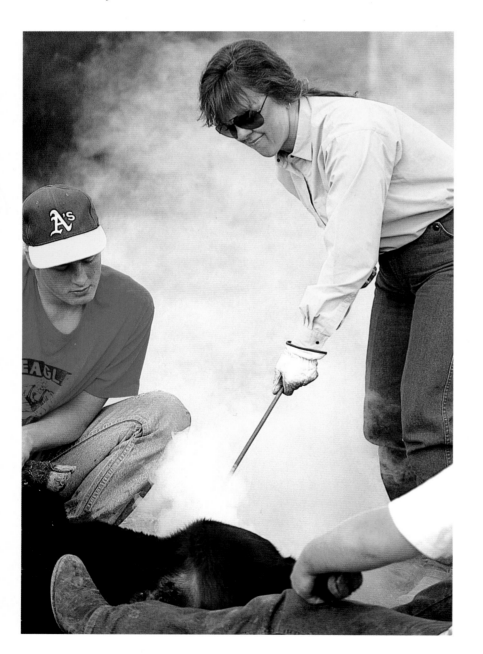

On other occasions, the sight of a "horseless carriage"—a car—would frighten the horse, and he would just take off down the road, pulling buggy and passengers behind him.

Horses remain important in the West, where cowhands still use them to round up cattle in the summer and cut out calves from the herd to be branded. Both horse and rider need great skill to isolate a lone calf from a milling herd. In frontier days, his horse was a cowboy's most precious possession, and even today, a cowhand has a special relationship with his horse. At rodeos, horse and rider work together to rope calves and perform equestrian skills before appreciative crowds. In other parts of the United States and Canada, many people enjoy riding horses for pleasure or in competitions. Some travelers ride horses on pack trips into the mountains. For every country child, riding a horse bareback across a summer meadow remains a delightful, almost primal, experience.

Fruits and Vegetables

As summer days pass, vegetables and fruits begin to ripen, and soon the harvesting of fresh foods begins. In some areas, berries are first— lush strawberries, blueberries, and raspberries plucked from plants and bushes and used for sweet shortcakes, cobblers, pies, and jams. Raspberries come the hardest, as these must be picked from thorny bushes, the thorns tearing at the skin and clothing of the eager picker, even as mosquitoes add their small torments to the scene. Yet there is nothing more delicious than fresh wild raspberries, gathered with difficulty and appreciated all the more for it.

Cowboys still ride the range in Wyoming, where cattle roam across vast landscapes in all seasons. In summer, cattle are rounded up and young calves are cut out from the herd so they can be branded.

Songs of old Texas waft through the air at a ranch outside Fort Worth. Many frontier ballads grew out of English or Spanish folk songs that cowboys sang to quiet the cattle or help fill long, lonely hours on the range.

One of my fondest childhood memories is going into a woodland thicket of wild raspberry bushes near our old family cottage in Ontario with my little pails and pots and filling them with berries. I proudly took my harvest home and over to our neighbor, Mrs. Drury, one of the world's great experts on making pies. She rolled out dough and filled pies—one for her family and one for mine—with the berries, and popped them into her stove, fueled with wood split by her husband's ax. As the pies baked, Mrs. Drury sat at her quilting frame on her porch, adding a few stitches to her work in progress, the tantalizing smell of the baking pies wafting over us. Soon I was walking home down the dirt country road, past breeze-blown cedar trees, a warm raspberry pie held carefully in my hands. This was it, one of the fondest of wholesome country pleasures that a child could feel on a sunny summer afternoon.

On other occasions, Mrs. Drury endowed me with fresh pies made from sour pale green apples picked from the tree beside her kitchen door. She also shared fresh lettuce and pungent onions, plucked from her garden, where, despite occasional raids from a raccoon, they grew thickly near nodding bluebells and tall pink phlox.

Summer gardens yield a multitude of delightful offerings—fresh yellow and green beans, tender peas, cabbages, carrots, and best of all, bright red tomatoes, ripened in the sun. Sweet corn turns to light gold and is sold at roadside stands, tempting travelers on the road to stop and buy. Watermelons, cantaloupes, and musk melons, too, ripen on the vine, and offer the prospect of cool refreshment. In orchards, pears and peaches swell to sweet succulence, waiting to be plucked. In country kitchens, these fresh ingredients go into meals—and into canning jars and freezing containers, so they can be eaten later in the year.

Country people say the water must be boiling on the stove before sweet corn is picked, so it can be cooked and eaten immediately. Any delay makes the corn starchy, they say—and I can attest to it, having participated in a corn-eating party at a farm in southern Michigan many years ago. The corn-on-the-cob we ate that day, rushed from field to pot to table, was the sweetest that could ever be. For dessert, we sat in the orchard under the trees and picked and ate fresh peaches and pears, dripping with juice.

Basketsful of scarlet strawberries will tempt palates when sprinkled on cool breakfast cereals, poured over steaming waffles, and heaped atop freshly baked shortcake.

Bursting with sweet juices, succulent strawberries are harvested at Four Corners Farm in Vermont. Visitors can pick their own at the farm, reaching amid dense and verdant leaves to pluck the enticing berries.

My friend Lionel, raised on a farm but now living in a city, says that one thing he misses greatly is really *good food*, food which is absolutely fresh. There *is* a difference he says, and there is nothing like the flavor of fresh chicken, good beef, fresh corn, and other completely fresh fruits and vegetables. For farm folk, such food is everyday fare, while city folk cannot know what they are missing.

Grains and Grasses

Fresh from the farm, red beets and leaf lettuce bring the taste of the country to tables in villages and towns. Truly fresh country food is more delicious than can be imagined by those who have not tasted it.

Summer sun makes grass, alfalfa, and clover flourish, ready to be cut for hay. Cutting, baling, and storing hay was once a time-consuming job involving pitchforks and heavy manual labor, but with today's mechanized equipment, the task is less daunting. Golden fields of grass are converted into sweeping lawns studded with rectangular bales, and increasingly, with huge rolled bales, which are more water-repellent than rectangular bales. The bales and rolls are gathered and stored, the energy of the sun captured to feed animals during the winter.

Wheat, too, is harvested, the season and exact timing dependent on the variety, location, and the weather. Throughout many states and parts of Canada, combines set out across seas of golden grain, reaping and threshing, gathering in abundant stores of this essential crop.

The sweetness of honey encourages a Connecticut beekeeper to take good care of his charges. In their endless quest for nectar, bees pollinate wild plants and crops, ensuring the continuing blessings of blooms and foliage across the countryside.

Sunset light gleams from a grain elevator in Montana, near mountains dusted with snow even in summer. All across the continent, wheat, soybeans, and other crops are safely stored in grain elevators before being transported by train to destinations near and far.

The rich produce of bountiful fields, ears of corn fill corn cribs silhouetted against the sunset in Michigan. Field corn feeds livestock, and corn oil and corn syrup flavor hundreds of foods that appear on our dining tables.

Metal roofing will shield this new barn in northern Vermont from the elements for many years. Neighbors cooperate in constructing the barn, as country people do all over North America.

Leaping high from limestone cliffs, swimmers plunge into Georgian Bay at Bruce Peninsula National Park, Ontario. Beneath the daring divers is a haunting grotto washed by the ice-blue waves of the Great Lakes. This region is a favorite of scuba divers, who explore natural underwater tunnels and old shipwrecks.

Diversions

When work is done, summer offers almost limitless opportunities for fun. Early in the summer, on the Fourth of July, parades, patriotic music, waving flags, and fireworks all mark the joy of celebrating America's Independence Day. At the end of July, Canadians enjoy the Civic Holiday weekend, three days of local fairs and festivities. Throughout the summer, large families gather at picnics to celebrate birthdays and family reunions. Everyone brings a contribution to the meal—fried chicken, salads, baked beans, cakes, and pies—and as many as forty or fifty people eat outdoors at picnic tables and laugh together with the pleasure of tasty food and family connectedness. For birthdays, special delights are a big cake and homemade ice cream, rich with the flavors of fresh cream and fruits.

In some rural areas, an annual town picnic or local fair draws folk from the region to the town square or park to eat together and strengthen their long-standing ties to one another. Competitions in hearty country-style activities such as log-splitting, wood-chopping, log-burling, load-pulling for teams of horses and for tractors, foot-racing, pig-roasting, and frog-jumping emphasize old-fashioned rural strength and good humor.

The unique lifeways of the Pennsylvania Dutch are honored at the Kutztown Fair in Pennsylvania. There, members of some Amish and Mennonite groups display their tempting baked goods, arts and crafts, and agricultural techniques to appreciative visitors from more worldly rural and urban traditions. The tidy bonnets, tight braids, and plain dresses of the Pennsylvania Dutch women contrast with the jeans, shorts, and flowing hair of the non-Amish fairgoers.

At county and state fairs, country people gather from miles around, bringing along some of their best produce and livestock, eager to display the results of their efforts and learn from one another. Finely groomed pigs, horses, sheep, beef cattle, dairy cattle, poultry, goats, and rabbits

Rushing water refreshes a bather at Sauble Falls, Ontario. For swimmers everywhere, summer's heat is washed away by cool lakes and streams, ponds, and pools.

Father and Mother, parents of children to whom they gave life and a sense of tradition, are honored at a cemetery in Belmont, Vermont. They symbolize all mothers and fathers, past and present, working to support their families and their countries.

A mossy gravestone erected in memory of a soldier of 1864 bespeaks the sorrow of war and premature demise. A tiny flag placed at the Vermont cemetery by modern hands honors the commitment of soldiers over the centuries.

Memories of yesteryear waft through a cemetery in Haddam, Connecticut. Gravestones remind the living of those who came before—people whose deeds helped shape the farms and towns of the North American continent.

Following page: Visitors explore the mysteries of a mountain lake in California's High Sierra. Melting snows run in icy streams down to the lake, filling it with chill water, and gush on down the mountainside to the flatlands below.

55

are assembled, oinking, neighing, bleating, lowing, and crowing, as their owners pitch aromatic hay and grain into their mangers and shovel manure from their stalls. Little boys and girls of 4-H clubs proudly lead huge cattle and pigs into show rings, and adolescents gracefully ride primped horses around an indoor course. Samples of field crops, canned fruits and vegetables artistically arranged in mason jars, baking, and needlework are all set out for judging. Blue and red ribbons abound, as prizes are awarded in a great number of categories. Ferris wheels, midway rides, food stalls, and carnival booths add to the fun, along with the selection of a Fair Queen to reign over the wholesome get-together. Country people participate in the fair not just for amusement, but to celebrate a way of life together, as they have for generations. For young people, it is here among their peers that many affirm their roles not only as willing helpers but as aspiring farmers of the future.

In the countryside, baseball games, golf, cycling, motorbiking, hiking, ballooning, bird-watching, and camping are popular summer diversions. For those with vacation time, hot weather pleasures include relaxing with a good book, walking down a shady path, lying in the

In a wetland lush with cattails along the Connecticut River, fishermen seek their aquatic prey with bow and arrow. A string tied to the arrow allows the successful archer to pull in his catch.

Spectacular snow-capped peaks of the Wallowa Mountains rise above forested hills and valley fields near the small town of Joseph in northeastern Oregon. In this scenic region shaped by glaciers, many farmers raise valuable herds of beef cattle.

Fluffy cotton candy delights young girls at the annual Village Fair in Wiarton, Ontario, on Canada's Civic Holiday weekend. The fair features a marathon, a boat race pitting floating bathtubs against rickety rafts, and a parade with bagpipers marching ahead of a pig-drawn cart.

Barns painted with advertisements have long adorned country landscapes across North America. A message from Mail Pouch tobacco on a barn in West Virginia reminds passersby of simpler times.

Fourth of July fireworks light up the sky, as onlookers perch atop a nearby structure in New York State. The brilliant explosions of sound and light remind holiday-makers of the nation's birth in the tempestuous Revolutionary War.

The spirit of 1776 is alive in the Fife and Drum Corps of Westbrook, Connecticut. The brightly garbed musicians march and play martial music of colonial times, bringing authenticity to modern Independence Day observances.

The Fourth of July is celebrated all across the United States, especially in country towns, with parades and other festivities. Here Boy Scouts and their leaders carry a huge American flag in proud procession.

Children eagerly await the arrival of marchers in the Fourth of July parade in a New England country town. Colorful crepe-paper streamers adorn their tricycles, while the children happily wave small American flags.

Red, white, and blue uniforms lend a patriotic air to the tunes of a marching band in Michigan. The stirring marches of John Philip Sousa are appropriate favorites on the Fourth of July. Sousa wrote many of his famous marches for the United States Marine Band, which he led in the late 1800s.

Solemnly bearing the flag of nation, a young member of the Fife a. Drum Corps stands at attention Westbrook, Connecticut. In many pa of the United States, young people pa ticipate in such groups, continuing w dignity the traditions of the countr

A horse hauls heavy blocks of cement in a pulling contest at Guilford, Vermont. Onlookers root for their favorites at this rural fair. Draft horses once supplied most of the power for jobs that heavy trucks and tractors do today.

Brawn, balance, and a good aim with an ax are what it takes to win the chopping competition at the Bridgewater Fair in Connecticut. Pioneer values of strength and willingness to do hard work are emphasized at many North American celebrations.

sun, swinging in a hammock, browsing at a flea market, bidding at an auction, visiting antique shops, climbing to the peaks of mountains, exploring deep caves, and backpacking into the wilderness. But on the hottest of summer days, nothing can compare with the joys of cool water.

Many choose fishing in smooth, quiet lakes or angling in cold streams with water tumbling over rocks; fly-fishing is an increasingly popular pursuit. Others prefer walking on an ocean beach washed by huge waves, the salt spray splashing all around and invigorating the air with a special energy. Some seek thrills in the surging surf, daring giant breakers to dash them or let them pass through the water safely. Adventurers find pleasure in canoes, rafts, and kayaks, paddling their way down rushing rivers, while others prefer boating in rowboats, motorboats, cruisers, and sailboats across lovely lakes. Windsurfing, jet-skiing, and riding tubes and water-skis over the waves can bring pleasure—as can swinging from a rope and jumping into the old swimming hole.

For people in the Midwest and Ontario, there is nothing like the Great Lakes, those gorgeous inland seas of fresh blue water alternately calm and topped by whitecaps, to cool the body and restore the spirit. For those who can brave the cold of these glacier-carved lakes, swimming and diving in their crystalline waters can be the ultimate summer pleasure.

Alas, summer does not last forever, not even in the beautiful countryside. The days gradually become shorter and cooler, and suddenly, as if in warning, a few leaves turn from green to gold. Summer's pleasures become memories that must last through the approaching seasons.

Old-fashioned high-wheeled bicycles roll in tandem in Madison, Connecticut. On high-wheelers—developed in the 1870s—each turn of the pedals rotates the big wheel once, allowing the bike to travel a long distance on each turn. Today's mountain-bikers and freestylers can hardly imagine cruising on these awkward vehicles.

At the annual frog-jumping contest in Bruce County, Ontario, a young girl sprays her frog with water to encourage him to leap. Contest rules forbid touching the competing frog with a finger or a stick—only blowing through a straw or spraying with water is allowed. The longest jump in each size category wins.

A happy winner, the girl proudly holds her hefty Canadian bullfrog. According to contest rules, after the competition, frogs are released back into their natural habitats, where they can croak and jump to their hearts' delight once again.

Old license plates attract a customer at a Massachusetts fleamarket. Rusty lanterns, musty tomes, chipped dishes, canned fruit, and antique jewelry are among the oddments offered for sale at outdoor markets.

A rough rider keeps his seat atop a bucking bull at a rodeo in Gardiner, Montana. Cowboy skills are kept sharp for rodeos, where big prizes can go to calf-ropers and bronco-riders. Clowns amuse rodeo crowds—and distract angry animals.

Treasures often appear at country markets, including furniture like this antique oak dresser with brass handles and knobs. Reflected in the mirror is a contented baby riding in a red wooden wagon shaded by a bright umbrella.

Previous page:
Muscles bulge and sawdust flies at the lumberjack
contest at the Bridgewater Fair in Connecticut.
The team that saws a slice off the hefty log in the
shortest time takes first place in the competition.

A sack race has kids hopping in a Kentucky
festival. Three-legged races, wheelbarrow
races, and other antics enliven the fair.
Light-hearted competition draws children
and parents together in the games, with
plenty of ribbons and small prizes for all.

Hubcaps galore bedazzle the eye at a fleamarket
in Englishtown, New Jersey. Need a hubcap for
your old Dart or Thunderbird? Maybe you'll
find it here—or at another outdoor market.

*Located in central Oregon, Rugged Smith Rocks challenges climbers
from all over the world who come to joust with nature. Less adventurous
visitors camp and hike among these intriguing formations.*

*Stone-grinding wheels have turned for more than a century at the
Butte Creek Mill in Oregon. Stream water powers the mill, which
daily produces stone ground flour for wholesome breads and pancakes.*

The Zest of Autumn

The air is crisp with autumn's coolness, brisk breezes blowing through leaves beginning to turn color. Deep greens give way to yellow, ocher, orange, and red, as fall creeps in upon the country landscape. By morning light, in early fall, the color changes are barely visible, as mists near the ground arise from the passage of cold air over earth still warm from summer. But as the sun rises high in the sky, it gleams clearly on luminous trees of gold and scarlet, standing in bright contrast to the evergreens around them.

In early fall the grass stays green, an emerald background for golden leaves fluttering down, a few and then a multitude, falling and carpeting the earth. The special scent of fallen leaves fills the air, sharp and refreshing to the nose. Dried leaves crunch underfoot.

In woodland glades, leaves drift down into flowing streams, where they are carried over rocks and under sheltering boughs by the swirling waters. Leaves drop into ponds and settle to the bottom, forming a layer beneath the water's surface to hide small water creatures. Leaves carpet the woodland floor, building up a layer of natural insulation beneath which small animals can burrow for protection from the elements and providing fertilizer for next spring's forest growth.

Squirrels scamper through the leaves, finding acorns topped with tiny caps, chestnuts, and walnuts, carrying them away and burying them for winter's meals, full of haste as autumn's days grow short. Fat woodchucks scurry into their burrows. Geese honk high above, flying in huge V formations, heading south to warmer climes. Flocks of swallows gather in chirping masses on wires and trees, assembling before their group flights to the south.

Aflame with autumn's vivid color, a sugar maple shades a country home in Massachusetts. Swings on the tree and on the porch have lulled both young and old amid the calm beauty of the New England countryside.

A fall mosaic of gold and green rises behind a grazing horse in a New England pasture. In this mountainous region, evergreens mingle with trees whose leaves turn bright with the season.

Shocks of cornstalks stand as sentinels on a field in Mifflin County, Pennsylvania. The ears of corn have long since been harvested by industrious Amish farm folk, working together as a family to secure their pious way of life.

Marigolds and mums still bloom, golden memorials to summer sun. At night light frost wilts soft leaves, but some hardy blooms survive to brighten fall days. Fluffy hydrangea blossoms—snowball flowers—dry from scented living white to rustling pale pink, prepared to stay on into winter. Tiny bittersweet berries of brilliant red-orange show themselves in country thickets and along the edges of fields, waiting to be gathered to adorn country tables and sideboards.

Harvest Time

The corn leaves in the fields dry from lush green to sandy brown and crackle in the wind. Farmers feel the ears for dryness, waiting and watching the weather. When autumn winds blow hard and the musty smell of harvest fills the air, the corn is finally dry enough to cut. America's most valuable crop, corn covers more land than any other crop in the United States. The golden kernels feed both livestock and people—corn, cornstarch, and corn syrup find their way into a thousand foods. In one form or another, corn makes up more of our diet than any other farm crop. Harvesting corn is very intense and critical work.

Work begins in predawn darkness and lasts until long after dark at night. Farmers drive combines into their fields, the big machines grasping the cornstalks, tearing off the ears, and scraping the kernels from the cobs. The shelled corn is hauled away in tractor-drawn wagons to be dried and stored. Other machines pick ear corn without shelling it, to be stored on the cobs in corncribs. In harvested fields, cornstalks are cut, raked, and round-baled to be used to feed and bed livestock during the winter months ahead.

Other crops are also ripe. In Illinois and other states, soybeans are harvested—rich sources of abundant protein and vegetable oil. In the United States, most wheat has already been harvested

Threshing wheat according to traditional methods, Amish farmers near Kutztown, Pennsylvania, toss grain stalks into a tried-and-true threshing machine. Grain and stalks are separated, one to feed farmers, and the other their animals.

by autumn—some 2.5 billion bushels of it, filling granaries to capacity. On the great plains of Saskatchewan, Manitoba, and Alberta huge crops of wheat are reaped in early fall—more than a billion bushels of golden grain destined to feed Canada and many other parts of the world. As long as the weather is dry, farmers can drive their combines late into the night, collecting the crops before a sudden squall of rain or hail might hit. Across the countryside of the United States and Canada, sunset light shines red through dust stirred up from fertile fields by combines, driven by hard-working farmers gathering in the valuable results of their year's labors. One of springtime's most important promises comes to fruition in the fall.

Where once a farmer walked behind a horse-drawn wagon, picking corn by hand and tossing it in at the rate of eighty bushels a day, today a farmer driving a combine can harvest four thousand bushels of corn in a good day. Yesteryear's farmers could hardly imagine the speed—and cost (between $80,000 and $200,000 for a combine, for example)— of today's agriculture. Farms are larger now, and yields are higher. A century ago, one farmer fed about ten people. Now he feeds more than sixty.

After a day's labors in Pennsylvania Dutch country, work horses rest in the gold of evening light. Behind them an abundant crop of corn is stored for use through-out the coming year.

Ears of amber corn, piled high in a Pennsylvania corn crib, are storehouses of the sun's energy, ready to provide food for humans and their animals. Native to the Americas, corn is the most valuable crop grown in the United States.

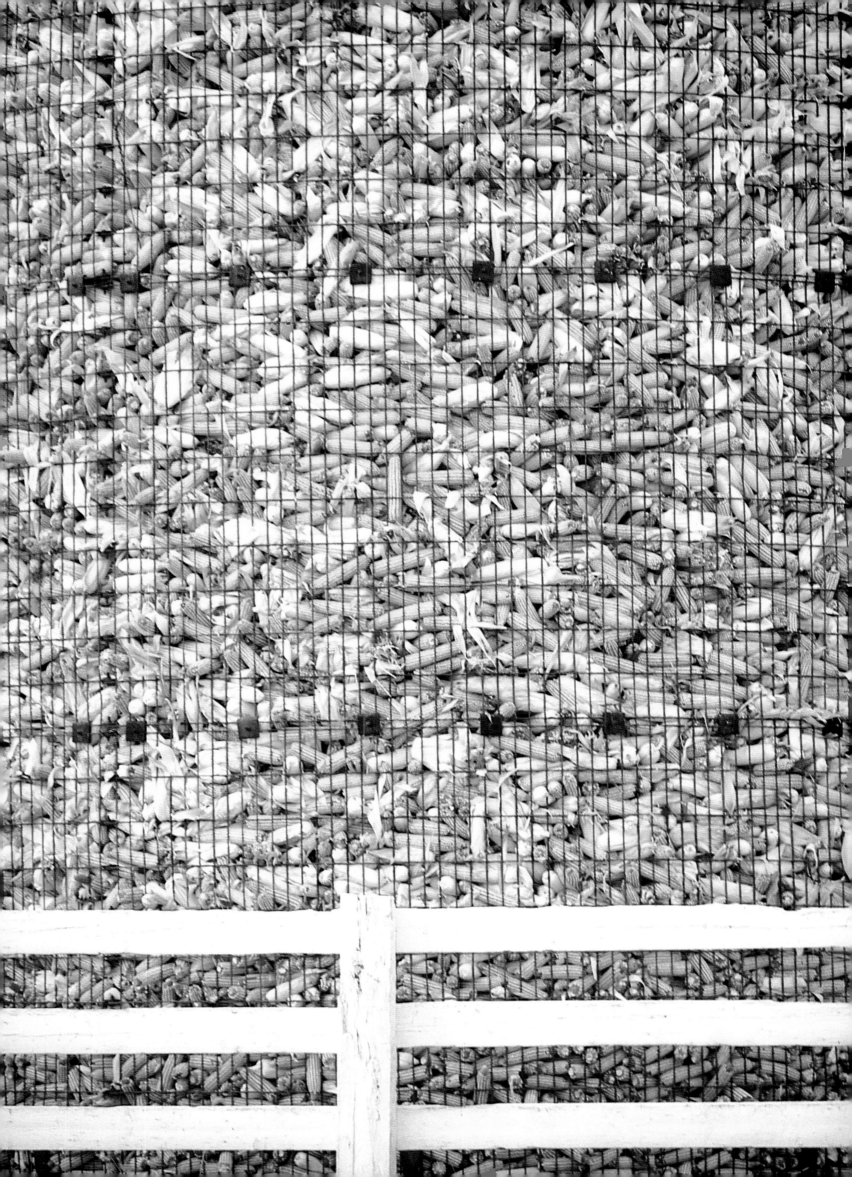

In the fall, the carefree days of summer give way to school days and the regimen of study. A school bus in Massachusetts stands ready to transport students with new shoes and books past golden trees to the schoolhouse door.

Fall brings gold to the Green Mountains of Vermont. Gilded trees are parted by a stream, its waters growing chillier with each passing autumn night.

In autumn, apple orchards are fragrant with ripening fruit, and fields are dotted with orange pumpkins. Visitors are often invited to pick their own, breathing in refreshing country air as they gather samples of nature's bounty to take home. Country markets and roadside stands are filled with mounds of vivid pumpkins, baskets of zesty apples, bunches of color-spattered Indian corn, bags of pecans and walnuts, piles of shapely squashes in a multitude of hues, pots of russet and yellow chrysanthemums, stacks of steaming apple pies, and gallons of freshly pressed tart apple cider.

A Leafy Tapestry

Arches of gold-leafed maples rise over country roads and town lanes, sheltering children on their way to school. For children, classroom routines have replaced the outdoor chores and free-flowing fun of summer. The students crowd into yellow school buses for long trips from farm to town, or they trudge, laughing, through layers of leaves on roads and sidewalks, tossing handfuls of leaves at each other as they go. On weekends they may join their parents on drives through cold-nipped areas where the autumn colors are especially beautiful. One such region is Vermont—where seventy percent of the land is covered by forest. There, amid picturesque mountains and valleys, the fall foliage is spectacular, drawing admirers from near and far.

As leaves pile themselves higher and higher under trees, billowing in the wind, drifting under hedges and over lawns, people start raking. Lawns would suffocate under such thick cover, so leaves are raked into small piles and huge heaps by families, working together in the invigorating air. Small children handle tiny rakes beside teenagers and parents with large ones, all joining in the spirit of autumn. Children delight in leaping and plunging into the piles of leaves, tossing

Pondering seasons past and seasons yet to come, a New England cyclist gazes into a fast-flowing stream. As summer ends and leaves fall, autumn is often a time for reflection and reassessment of the direction of one's life.

A treasured antique car rests in the shelter of a canopy of scarlet and gold in New York state. Its wheels have rolled down many country roads through decades of history.

Sheltered in the lee of a stone fence and spared the bite of frost, flowers still bloom at Shelburne Falls, Massachusetts. Nearby trees have turned to gold, and maple leaves have fallen, anticipating the fate awaiting even these hardy blossoms.

Previous page:
Amidst the rich colors of
autumn, a covered bridge
crosses a stream in the
White Mountains of New
Hampshire. To save labor
and lumber, many New
England bridges were cov-
ered to protect the wooden
planking from the elements.
As an extra benefit, courting
couples could sometimes find
a moment alone under the
shelter of the covered bridge.

them high, fighting mock battles, building ephemeral forts, pretending to sleep in soft rustic beds of nature's creation. Leaf-blowers are called into service, moving the mounds of leaves off lawns and gardens and into areas where they can be left or burned.

The fires are lit, and then the smoky scent of burning leaves—the quintessential aroma of autumn—drifts through the air. It is a strong smell that cannot be ignored. For some, it chokes the breathing and irritates the nose, but for most, it is delightful, evoking strong memories of childhood and youth, of the new school year, exuberant football games, a sidelong glance in school from a favorite boy or girl, a shy walk down a wooded lane with that special person, parties with cider and doughnuts, a hayride under a harvest moon, and perhaps a kiss under a tree whose branches are half-bare yet still half-clothed in golden leaves.

A task begun in summer takes on new urgency now—cutting firewood. The buzzing of chain saws resounds from woodlots as hardwood trees are felled and sliced into stove-sized lengths. Delivered to sideyards, the wood is split and stacked into large neat piles, ready to warm hearths in the cold months ahead.

A golden maple announces autumn at a dairy farm
in Holland, Vermont, near the Canadian border.
Verdant pastures and tranquil ponds still show summer's
warmth, even as fall creeps up upon the land. Benches
provide seating for visitors to the much-admired farm.

Fall foliage surrounds a country home in a quiet corner of
New England. Years of changing seasons have weathered the
wood on house and fence to a graceful silver. Up and down
this lane residents of the home and their visitors have trav-
eled countless times, carrying out life's labors and celebrations.

A Halloween tableau features a jack-o'-lantern carved from a fresh pumpkin. Costumed children, trick-or-treating in the dark of Halloween night, will see his eyes and scary mouth aglow with the light of a candle burning inside his hollow head.

Scarecrows whimsically guard frost-wilted fields in southern Vermont. Pumpkins and shocks of corn stalks are unmistakable markers of autumn's arrival.

Halloween

Preparations begin for Halloween, the October festival when ghosts and witches prowl the countryside by the light of flickering jack-o'-lanterns. The holiday is rooted in the ancient Celtic festival of Samhain, which marked the beginning of the season of cold, darkness, and decay. Two thousand years ago, the Celts believed that the lord of death allowed the souls of the dead to return to their earthly homes for this one evening, October 31. Much later, in the ninth century, the church established All Saints' Day on November 1 and celebrated mass the evening before—All Hallow Even. Without realizing it, today's Halloween revelers enjoy some very ancient customs, though less in reverence than in good fun.

Young people scour out big round pumpkins and help parents carve horrendous features in the rind. A candle set inside gives off an orange glow, the flame gleaming out through wicked eyes and snaggle-toothed mouth, as if from the severed head of a demon. Fake skeletons and black cats dance in windows, and spooky white-sheeted ghosts hang from trees. Children dress up in costumes of all kinds, ranging from fairy princesses, knights, and television characters to blood-sucking Draculas, pointy-capped witches, and Frankenstein's monsters.

In rural areas where houses are far apart, children celebrate Halloween at school parties. In towns where houses are close together, masked and costumed youngsters flit about in the evening darkness, swooping from house to house over fallen leaves to trick-or-treat, begging for candy at each door. Later, they count their loot like pirate kings sifting through piles of golden coins—chocolate bars, candy corn, candy kisses, pennies, apples, popcorn, and a hundred other delectations designed to decay their teeth and gladden their hearts. Teenagers, for whom such antics seem too childish, may trick or treat for UNICEF, seeking cash donations in official orange and black cartons to help children in far-off countries.

Some pranksters spray houses with shaving cream, wind streamers around yards, toss eggs at windows, push over tombstones, and smash pumpkins on the road. In days gone by, teenage boys would lie in wait until a man went into his outhouse, then rush up and push the privy over onto its door, so that the hapless victim was trapped inside.

Halloween remains a night when youngsters can live their fantasies of "who they want to be," beautiful queen or dangerous monster, Mickey Mouse or Captain Kirk, when some rules of decorum are in abeyance, and all can acknowledge the changing of the season.

Pumpkins grow on trailing green-leafed vines on a Michigan farm, their orange tones reflected in the barns behind them. Long before the arrival of European settlers, Native Americans cultivated pumpkins to a high degree of perfection.

As Halloween approaches, children speak of pumpkins and imaginative costumes at rural Clayville on the central Illinois prairie. Clusters of Indian corn dry on a split-rail fence behind them. A century and a half ago, young Abraham Lincoln built similar fences at the nearby village of New Salem.

OUR OWN
JUST PICKED
INDIAN
CORN 2.50

DELICATA
.29 lb

BUTTERNUT
.29 lb

Pumpkins abound outside a country store in Pennsylvania Dutch country. Many of these pumpkins will wind up as jack-o'-lanterns, while others will provide tasty filling for spicy pumpkin pies.

Baskets full of tangy apples line the shelves at a New England country market. The bounty of North America's orchards fills fresh-baked apple pies and cider jugs, adding zest to autumn meals.

Colorful Indian corn along with shapely squashes are offered for sale at a country vegetable market. The bunches of corn will decorate doorways, while the squash will be baked with butter and brought steaming to the dinner table.

Hunting

Autumn is also the season of hunting. Some people abhor this sport, but hunters find it gratifying to stalk pheasants, quail, deer, antelope, elk, and even moose and bear through grass and trees, and many take pleasure in spending chilly early morning hours in a cramped blind beside a pond to shoot at ducks. Hunters enjoy being immersed in the countryside, walking over the land, being in tune with the wild animals, and, ultimately, bringing meat home for the family. Many hunters work with dogs, who, with their fine sense of smell, become allies of the humans against the prey animals. Some hunters use bows and arrows. For a hunter, there is a feeling of tremendous accomplishment when he comes home with his full quota of pheasants or ducks, or with his legally allowed deer strapped to the front of his car, and he and his family savor the meat as long as it lasts. To those who object to hunting, a hunter replies that without culling, many deer would die of starvation during the harsh winter, and furthermore, anyone who is not a vegetarian eats animals that have been killed, whether by himself or by someone else acting for him.

Climbing over a farm fence in Michigan, a boy hands his gun to his father to hold. Hunting brings father and son together as they explore fall fields and woods in their quest for pheasants to bring home to the family larder.

Successful in his hunt for a ring-necked pheasant, a Nebraska hunter praises his helpful dog. Hunting dogs work closely with their owners, using their sensitive sense of smell to locate and retrieve birds.

Preparing for the family celebration of Thanksgiving, a little boy helps his mother and grandmother cut out cookies in Grandma's country kitchen.

A family happily gathers to share a deliciously browned Thanksgiving turkey. Traditional harvest fare draws friends and relatives together to give thanks, feast, and enjoy each other's company.

Celebrations

In fall, as in other seasons, evenings bring out the sounds of country music. When time permits, country people gather to play the fiddle and guitar and to dance, their spirits lifted by the rhythmic sounds and motion and, for some, by foaming pitchers of cold beer. Many enjoy square dancing, dressed in jeans and full skirts, responding to the caller's commands to swirl about the floor in intricate maneuvers.

Finally, the fields lie fallow, broken corn stalks rustling in the cold wind, deer nibbling on the shreds. Heavy frosts and light snow have killed all vestiges of vegetation, save that on evergreens. On maples and oaks, only a few shriveled brown leaves cling to bare branches, silhouetted against a steel-gray sky. Many farm animals have been collected in their pens and barns. The harvest is safely in, and outdoor work diminishes. Thanksgiving is in the air. The bounty of the harvest is celebrated—in October in Canada and in November in the United States—a day of families joining together for fun and feasting.

In the warm kitchen, succulent, savory foods are brewing, sending delicious smells throughout the house. In the dining room, the table is covered with a treasured tablecloth and laid with family dishes and silverware. The phone rings frequently, and people begin to arrive.

Children, grandchildren, parents, grandparents, cousins, and dear friends all gather at the table, ready to devour the Thanksgiving feast. Dad sharpens his carving knife, and Mom brings out the turkey, roasted crispy and golden, stuffed with dressing. More dishes follow—baked potatoes, sweet potatoes, cranberry sauce, salad, carrots, green beans, hot rolls, gravy, pickled beets, sweet cucumber pickles, corn relish—the list is almost endless.

All hold hands to say the blessing. And then, amid great talk and chatter, the eating begins, each morsel savored. The meal is topped off with fresh-baked pies—mincemeat, apple, pumpkin, and peach—each more delicious than the next. All who have gathered take pleasure in being together, proudly enjoying the fruits of the land and their labors. As night falls, within the warm home all are content, and no one is bothered by the sounds of cold winds whistling outdoors across the countryside.

Autumn leaves tossed high shower fall fun on happy children. Raking leaves is a chore that can be shared by young and old, working and playing together in the brisk air.

Following page:
White snow blankets the ground
and highlights autumnal trees in
New England. A country building
constructed sturdily of stone
shelters warmth and love within.

Mowing dried cornstalks with the help of his mule
team, an Amish farmer of Lancaster, Pennsylvania,
prepares for cold weather. The stalks are used for bedding
and fodder for farm animals during the long winter.

Dawn light gleams through
autumn mists on a wood-
land lake in New England.
Pines are reflected in the
still, unrippled waters, not
yet frozen in the cooling air.

The Magic of Winter

Winter's light is often pale, filtered through gray clouds and falling snowflakes before it strikes the frozen ground. Yet sometimes the winter sun is brilliant, with no leaves on trees and bushes to deflect its rays, shining bright on fawn-colored grass and barren branches dusted with white snow. Yet whether pale or bright, winter's light does not last long. Evening comes early now, and the dark of night descends quickly as winter's hand is felt upon the land.

Country Comforts

Ever aware of the weather and its impact on them, country people are well prepared for the new season. Fireplaces and chimney flues are clean, hearths are swept, windows caulked, roofs repaired, door latches firm, hay stores put up, and larders full.

In Canada and northern regions of the United States, woolen sweaters, coats, scarves, and mittens are taken from cedar chests and kept near at hand in bedroom and hall closets. Beds are made up with fuzzy flannel sheets and warm blankets topped with handsewn quilts.

Winter warns of its approach with frosts and flurries, plummeting temperatures, and crusts of ice. Then comes the snow, falling thickly, countless snowflakes drifting, tumbling, softly blanketing the earth with white. Bare branches and evergreen boughs are covered and bend under its soft weight. Roofs of houses and barns are mantled in white, and windows are festooned with ferns and feathers of frost covering the cold panes. The morning light glints from ice crystals on frozen

White silence covers a cemetery in Old Bennington, Vermont. Snow adorns gravestones and the fence around them, while a bright American flag enlivens the quiet scene.

Feathers of frost adorn a windowpane, thin barrier between the chill of the wintry outdoors and the warmth of life inside. Ice forms on the glass as contrasting temperatures meet, taking on the beautiful shapes of crystal plumes.

Little white lights sparkle on a traditional New England Christmas tree, inviting family and friends to come from near and far to celebrate the holidays together.

The pink glow of sunset highlights wintry mountain tops. Soft white snow spreads peace over the quiet country landscape, silently awaiting the rebirth of spring.

When the Italian Renaissance artist Raphael painted this nobleman's portrait in 1516, he never imagined it would appear centuries later on the side of a Michigan barn, framed by tall grasses crunchy with snow.

Fortunate in finding a snack beneath the snow, a deer grazes in a piney woods in Montana. When winter weather is severe, scarcity of fodder often causes hardship for deer, elk, and antelope.

grass and illuminates in the snow the tiny tracks of mice and sparrows and the larger tracings left by rabbits, foxes, and deer.

The first person up on a cold morning rushes to the black cast-iron stove to start the fire. She opens the heavy stove door, strikes a wooden match to light the kindling, and its quick blaze catches the logs on fire, sending welcome warmth out into the room. She adjusts the stovepipe damper, allowing the woodsmoke to billow out the chimney high above, and turns to making breakfast for the family.

For most, these elemental moments with wood and fire and air have been replaced by a quick turn of the dial on a thermostat linked to an electric or oil-fueled furnace. But most country people can remember the good feeling of holding their cold hands close to a hot iron stove to drive away winter's chill and restore circulation to their fingers.

Most can also remember washing up with well water, hauled in buckets from the hand pump in the yard to the kitchen. On winter nights, a thin layer of ice often formed on the water in the buckets near the kitchen sink. In the days before plumbing became common in country homes, a dipper always hung on a nail beside the bucket, to be used for the family to drink from, or to dip water for the washbowl. In winter, hot water from the stove was always added to the cold water in the china or enamel washbowl till it was just the right warmth to cleanse the face and hands. There was nothing like a brisk face-washing with double handfuls of water from the washbowl to wake a person up in the morning.

The trip to the outhouse on a cold winter morning was also a quick waker-upper. A fast run down the snowy path was followed by a cold blast of wind up the privy hole—guaranteed to drive away the last vestiges of sleepiness! Anyone who has never rushed through ice and snow to a freezing outhouse does not fully realize what a luxury a warm bathroom is. Also, before plumbing, in case someone had not been able to make it out during the night, the chamber pots had to be emptied each morning and cold well water pumped into them to clean them out.

With summer's pasture denied to them, penned-up livestock need deliveries of fodder. Before they themselves can eat, farm folk must tend to the animals, providing food to hogs and cattle,

A dark horse peers from its stable yard at Belmont, Vermont, where thick snow reflects bright sunlight. White-blanketed mountains rise behind him.

horses and poultry. Dogs and cats stick even closer than usual to their people, knowing that they are the source of welcome warmth and food.

Even wild creatures depend on human kindness for their meals on days of ice and snow. Ears of corn set out for squirrels are quickly chewed bare, and birdfeeders filled with seeds and suet are emptied within minutes. Chickadees, cardinals, sparrows, doves, woodpeckers, and a multitude of other birds derive essential sustenance through the continuing thoughtfulness of country people.

Joys of Snow

After a night's snowfall, country lanes must be plowed and shoveled so people can go about their daily business. Some farms are well equipped with plows to clear away the snow, while others depend on hand labor to make walks and driveways passable. All in the family, including children, bend to this invigorating task, delighting in the feel of powdery crystals blowing across their faces as they toss snow from one place to another.

Before the ways are cleared, some children must leave for school, stepping deep into snowdrifts that reach to the tops of their boots. A small child, bundled up warm in winter coat, mittens, leggings, scarf, hat, woolen socks, and boots, feels a unique sense of immersion in the winter elements as he plunges into snowdrifts along the road or in a field, deliberately challenging lumps of snow to fall inside his boots.

The hours of school are spent in classrooms lit with sunlight reflected from the white snow outside. Some students stay after class to practice basketball or volleyball, while others dash straight off to enjoy the snow.

Children pack sun-warmed snow between their hands and hurl snowballs at each other. They use three

A beautiful coverlet of snow fallen during the night envelops a country landscape. Morning light reveals soft cold tufts of snow on every branch and twig.

A white-tailed deer lifts her head to scan a misty white New England landscape. Frosty grass and corn stubble help sustain the deer in this season of ice and snow.

Ice-fishing in Alger County, Michigan, yields an impressive catch — a glossy northern pike. Good eating lies ahead for the angler, whose patience has paid off.

Bending together to their wintry task, family members shovel deep snow drifts from their farm lane outside Dexter, Michigan. Main roads are plowed by counties and municipalities, but private lanes and roads are cleared by owners themselves.

Strolling through a snowy landscape is made easier with snowshoes — invented long ago by North American Indians. In some parts of Canada, members of snowshoe clubs glide together over the surface of deep snow.

snowballs to start three rolls, and soon they have a snowman made of huge balls of snow, an appealing and long-lasting presence in the front yard outside the house.

They rush to the barn or garage to find their sleds and toboggans, and soon the best slopes are covered with colorfully capped youngsters swiftly swooping downhill. Each run is followed by a long trek up the hill and yet another thrilling swoosh down the slick white slope. In some states and provinces, specially constructed toboggan runs draw groups of families and friends who hug each other close as they shoot down the ramp at great speed. In some rural areas, a few people are privileged to drive through snowy woods in a horse-drawn sleigh, bundled tightly under a warm blanket in the frigid air, the jingling of the sleighbells enhancing the delight of the occasion.

When the cold has had time to set in deeply, ponds and lakes freeze over with ice thick enough to bear the weight of people and even vehicles. Skaters skim on silvery blades over the surface of the frozen water, gracefully turning and spinning like snowflakes in the wind. Optimistic ice-fishermen cut several holes in the thick ice, drop in baited lines, and wait patiently for a bite, hoping to haul home fresh fish for supper.

In Vermont, New Hampshire, upstate New York, Colorado, Idaho, and many other hilly and mountainous regions, deep snow means just one important thing to many people: skiing. City and country people alike take to woodland trails for cross-country skiing, and they cluster at ski lifts to be carried to the top of mountains for down-hill skiing. With long, thin slats strapped to their well-booted feet, the skiers revel in their sport, as they speed down trails and schuss down slopes, feeling at one with the snowy elements.

Some enjoy tramping through snowy landscapes with snowshoes, webbed contraptions that keep the walker from plunging through the surface of deep snow. Others leap onto snowmobiles to roar across the snow, both for work and pleasure. Derided by some nature lovers as destructive of the peace of nature, snowmobiles have become an almost indispensable tool for many country people, especially those living in the far north.

Happily tired from their exertions in the snow and ice, people come inside to warm themselves beside a roaring fire in the fireplace and drink mugs of warm cocoa and coffee. Hearty sandwiches and bowls of hot soup refuel exhausted bodies for yet another bout of work or play in the frigid winter air. The fragrance of wood smoke wafts through the atmosphere, adding to the contentment of the season.

Cross-country skiers take to the trails in snowy Stowe, Vermont. Bundled up and safely tucked into his father's backpack carrier, a tiny passenger enjoys the wintry ride.

schussing down the slopes at Sugarbush, Vermont, a skier flies over the snow. Trees rise above, frosted with ice crystals and snowflakes. For skiers, nothing surpasses the invigoration of a fast downhill run.

A small wreath of
evergreen in the
window welcomes
visitors to this cozy
New England home.
Plants growing
inside the warm
house beckon to the
dormant plants
in the cold outdoors.

One can almost hear
the carols sung by
these old-fashioned
singers in a Christmas
display at Lenox,
Massachusetts.
Evergreen roping
and small trees
festooned with scarlet
ribbons suggest the
joy of the season.

Returning from the
snow-filled woods,
a couple carry their
balsam fir home
to adorn their parlor
for the holidays.

Previous page:
Sleigh bells jingle merrily as a team of
horses pulls riders on a sleigh through
woods in Connecticut. Capturing the fun
of yesteryear, the ride leaves passengers
with tingling faces and happy memories.

Holiday magic glows from the colored lights on
an outdoor tree at Stockbridge, Massachusetts.
Surrounded by the blue of night and reflected
in the snow, the lights spark thoughts of
harmony between nature and humanity.

The spirit of the holidays is evoked in
this classic nativity scene in a country
setting in New York state, expressing
hope for future happiness on earth.

Holiday Festivities

As the month of December begins, people in the countryside prepare for the great winter festival of Christmas. The celebration falls within days of the Winter Solstice, the moment when the days are the shortest in the year, after which they start to lengthen, signaling the start of a new cycle of the seasons. This is one of the busiest and happiest periods of the year.

Across the United States and Canada, holiday observances vary, reflecting the diverse national origins of the people. Traditions brought from many countries mingle with practices developed here, adding special meaning to the holiday. For all—including for those celebrating the Jewish holiday of Chanukah—there is an element of family love, mixed with the spirit of giving.

Gifts are crafted, cards are sent, red ribbons tied. Mistletoe, holly, and evergreens are strung. Nativity scenes, lighted candles, and figures of Santa Claus, reindeer, and carolers are displayed. Little lights twinkle in country towns and on country houses, announcing to all who pass by the joy of the season.

Perhaps most beautiful are snowy outdoor Christmas trees, decorated with strings of multicolored lights, twinkling in the darkness, reflected in the snow. In this combination of winter's natural wonderland adorned with festival lights the magic of Christmas is revealed.

Country families join together to walk through the woods to select a balsam or a pine tree for the holiday. Having found just the tree they want, they cut it down, carry it home, and set it up inside. With carols playing in the background, children and adults adorn the tree with glittering lights, treasured family ornaments, strings of cranberries,

His face bright with holiday excitement, a young boy opens a very special present. Long-hoped-for gifts bring happiness to children at this cheerful season.

swags of tinsel, and, atop it all, a shining star. As the tree warms, it perfumes the house with the fragrant scent of the forest.

Christmas Eve and Christmas Day are special times for families, with far-flung relatives arriving to spend the holiday at home. Candles glow in the window, lighting the way for guests as they come up the snow-dusted walk. Some attend Christmas Eve services at the church in town, while others worship on Christmas morning. Brightly wrapped gifts are stacked under the tree—some brought by Santa Claus, others by members of the family—and opened amid rejoicing and good cheer. At Christmas dinner, sharing in an abundance of good food and drink further draws families together.

Beside a fire glowing on the hearth, children snuggle in their parents' laps to hear bedtime stories. The world outside is cold, but all within the cozy shelter of the home feel only warmth.

Ring in the New

The New Year brings with it the prospect of the end of winter and a new cycle of life in the country. Beneath the blanket of snow covering the ground, plants lie dormant, ready to start their growth as soon as the weather turns warm. Each evening, as the sun sets, it highlights wintry trees, icy ponds, and snowy fields and hills in its rosy light, hinting at the approaching rebirth of spring.

A rocking chair and mother's arms spell security to a little girl, as mother and child read a children's story. Winter's chill is banished from the home, where the warmth of family love pervades.

The warm glow of a wood fire on the hearth keeps sisters comfortable on a winter day. Playing a children's card game indoors is a cozy alternative to frolicking in the snow outside.

A fantasy castle created of petrified wood shimmers with Christmas radiance in McAllen, Texas. The unique structure is illuminated every year, continuing a neighborhood tradition in this town near the Rio Grande.

*White country church and colonial-style houses blend with their
winter coat of snow in Belmont, Vermont. In country towns like this,
valued ways of life and beauty continue from past to present.*

*An elegant swan lends life and beauty to a winter
scene in Washington, Connecticut. The white-
plumed bird is gracefully at home amid snow and ice.*

Photo Credits